Love Songs *from the* Heart

———— Book 2 ————

Love Songs *from the* Heart

A Collection of Inspirational Thoughts and Feelings on Love and Life!

———— Book 2 ————

DENNIS NICOMEDE

iUniverse, Inc.
New York   Bloomington

Love Songs From The Heart

Book 2

A Collection of Inspirational
Thoughts and Feelings on Love and Life!

iUniverse books may be ordered through booksellers or by contacting:

iUniverse
1663 Liberty Drive
Bloomington, IN 47403
www.iuniverse.com
1-800-Authors (1-800-288-4677)

ISBN: 978-1-4401-0156-4 (pbk)
ISBN: 978-1-4401-0157-1 (ebk)

Registration No.: TXu 1-595-342

Year of Copyright: 2008

Printed in the United States of America

Library of Congress Control Number: 2008941763

iUniverse rev. date: 2/11/2009

DEDICATION

I humbly dedicate this book, first and foremost, to the Divine Source from which all flows, and secondly to all my universal brothers and sisters of love and truth.

This book was not written for great writers and poets but rather for the common man or woman with an open heart and an ear for the Spirit!

Contents

ACKNOWLEDGMENT

I wish to acknowledge the Divine Source from which this work came and the administering spirits that helped bring this book to life.

I also acknowledge my family, friends and all artisans, musicians, writers, poets, dancers and the beautiful humanitarians who have touched so many lives, including my own, with their Truth, Beauty, Wonder and Goodness. The list is just too numerous to mention but I thank you all.

And most of all, I want to thank my loving wife and partner, Jeanne, without whose love and effort this book would still be on bits and scraps of paper from New York to L.A.

Be still and allow True Spirit to move or stir.

And when the time's right,

True Spirit will emerge triumphantly!

LOVE'S ESSENCE

I love you deeply.
Oh, so deeply.
And I'm so sorry to have to watch
Yet another dream slip away.

There were 10,000 more songs to share
A hundred million words yet to write
And a lifetime of nights to share
in the expression of love
That only true union can bring.

My love for you was so fine and pure
Now it lays shattered on the ground like
so many pieces of broken crystal.
Human hearts are never to be played with
But truly only to be gently held, rocked
and caressed as a newborn babe.

And I'll continue to love deeply and passionately
Over and over again
Until I learn the fullness of Love's Essence
Or
The Essence of Love!

OUR PROCESS HOME

How amazing to finally see
That all the heartaches and tears we've shed for others
Now turns into our joy and supreme Love.

I give thanks to them all
Each and every one
Who have helped us get to this point of sweet union.
This union of two, becoming one!

These words I write in honor of all of us
In our process home.

THE MIRROR'S REFLECTION

So many people walk by each day.
So varied are they in size, shape and color.
Some attractive by the beauty of their form,
Some attractive by their sheer force of being.

I try to look at them all.
Some look away, some look down.
Some look at me in return.
And the things I see,
Oh, the things I see in their eyes...

Such love and peace
Such warmth and kindness
Such freedom and ease
Such pain and hurt
Such guilt and remorse
Such anger and hatred
Such apathy and disdain.

And then like the cleansing rain,
There's the smiles of wonderment and play
on the angelic faces of the children.
Oh, the beautiful children!

And there I stand
Stunned by the mirror's reflection.

ONCE IN A BLUE MOON

It was not only a rare Blue Moon,
It was as close to Mother Earth as it would be all year.
I was over-powered by its brilliance.
Rippling waves of moonlight washed over
me like the healing hands of my lover.
I was mesmerized by its spiritual pull.
It stood silently beckoning me home.
Wrapping me up in its glow,
Like a mother cradles her young.
Without hesitation or thought,
I fell soul first into its beauty.
I sat bathed in things that were,
And golden images of things to come.
In one eternal moment after another
Paradise just in sight
And hope on the rise
As the fruits of freedom and worship filled my being.

And some say it only happens once in a Blue Moon.
I say they lie.

When you dress up, you're beautiful.
But when you laugh or smile and it comes out naturally,
Your beauty is in your beingness.
It comes from your soul.

THE HEALING

Blessed Father,

Please help heal these growing pains we're
going through...
    The pain of a cherished love left behind.
    The pain of love's betrayal.
    The pain of love's refrain.
    The pain of broken promises and shattered dreams.
    The pain of uncertainty in what seemed so certain.
    The pain of letting go of the Belief in Love
    To rise to the level of True Faith in Love.

Oh Blessed Father, I'll ask no more,
But rather whole-heartedly put my Faith and Trust in *You,*
By asking, "Not my will, but Yours be done."

                In Your name...from your children.

UNEXPLORED TERRITORY

Father,
Let me try to thank you for the goodness
You've put in my heart,
The beauty You allow me to see,
The truth that daily rings inside of me,
The love You've brought my way,
For Your presence each and every day,
To guide and light my way.
As You wrap me in this, Your willing vortex
of angel wings and spirits bright.

THE STREAM OF LIFE

Blessed morning unfolds
Like a newborn baby entering the world.
As I sit wrapped in a magical blanket
of ahh and bewilderment,
Not knowing if this is real
Or if I'm still walking the dream.

I'm so overwhelmed in a sea of spiritual emotion,
That I don't know whether to kneel or worship
Or just sit here and cry for all the
love I've just been given.
In just –
The light from her eyes
The glow of her smile
The strength of her words
The power of her faith
The life in her touch.

Dare I move and break the spell?
Dare I close my eyes and lose the vision?
Dare I question and let doubt in?
Dare I have the strength to hold
on tight and just love her,
As we gently slip into the stream of Life!

A COUNTRY WITHIN A COUNTRY

Ahh to be in that country!
That country that feels like home.
That country that feels so safe.
That country that brings such peace.

That country that's without hate, hurt or pain.
That country that breeds freedom, fairness,
        and openness.
That country that's awash in spark, flame, and desire.
That country that's bathed in Love, Light, and Hope.

That country that feels so damned real.
That country I roam in when I'm held in your embrace,
        ...When I'm stunned by your touch,
                ...When I'm moved by your kiss,
                        ...When I'm joined by your spirit.

I'm lost in your country...
That country within a country.

                    – Always –

THE RELEASE OF LOVE

After one of the greatest unions of our lives,
She asks me if I would affirm the
release of the deep river of love
that's bound within her.

As I pray and heal her while she sleeps
the sleep of a thousand years,
I love her call for union,
As I laugh quietly to myself.

Know the Truth,
That one need but ask from the heart
And all is freely given.
As one takes the first step to find the Father,
He has found Him.
For the Father was never lost,
But quietly waiting to be sincerely requested.

I love her for reasons only true love knows.
I've never been more filled with the feeling and
understanding of the presence of Love
Then these precious moments since we touched.
I will pray and share my love with her
'Til morning's light and red dots fading.

Resistance is always met with force.

TOTAL BEINGNESS

Jeanne,
Sorry I can't settle
For just being a Nice Guy,
A Good Man –
I want to Be, Must Be
The Total Being that I am—
I want to be the Fullness of the Man I Am—
In hopes of bringing out
The total Woman that You are—
Turn away or turn to me!
The choice, as always, is yours
But this is the *spark* of Life
And the *feelings* you've brought to me!

In Great Honor and Respect.

ONE STEP AT A TIME

Roses are red and violets are blue,
Moonbeams are golden and
so are you.

I'm not checking in and
I'm not checking out,
Now you know what it's all about.

One step at a time and
you're never out of line.

Love is Eternal –
Love is Life –
Love Is.

FOR EVERY MAN

It's hard to get in touch with your soul if you can't let go.
You've got to let go of the image and just be.
Play with what you feel inside –
Your basic blocks of understanding.

Then begin to glide up to Spirit –
Spiritual understanding.
Then just kneel, man, kneel!
And be quiet, like calm waters.
And like the spring flower, you'll begin to open up
And reach for all the light you can take in.
It'll be as mystical as the moments when you
just break out in tears of joy and worship.
And at that moment, you'll know.
You'll know just how truly great we
little creatures can be.

Thank you Father.

MEN ARE – I AM

Men are often quiet and reserved with their feelings.
But we are also moved and touched
by the sweet and tender touch of Love.
A human touch that reaches into
the very soul of their being.

Don't try to generalize all men
by the meter of the one you're with.
Accept him, if you can,
For who he is –
No more - No less.
But do love and assist in his growth
As he should yours.

What a two-way street this road we call Life is!
Why hate when you can give thanks
for moments shared and moments spent.

Always in memory of
And hope for.

HO TA HAY

IT'S A BEAUTIFUL DAY

HOW MUCH

How much life can be seen?
How much life can be felt?
How much life can be embraced?
How much life can be shared?
How much life can be lived?
How much life can be without Love?
Not much!
Not much at all!

SOME PEOPLE

Some people say they believe in the Oneness
from which all reality manifests...
In the "I AM" of the "I AM,"
In their presence in reality,
That they truly are real,
And they come from that which Is,
In the respect of one another,
In the power of true love, real love, Divine Love,
In the sanctity of everyone's process
of healing themselves,
In the mystical magic lying just beyond sight,
In the miracle of birth,
In the visions of smoke,
In the creation of thought,
In the Divine Purpose of the Universe—
Some people say they Believe.
Some really DO!

PRE-GLIMPSE OF DAWN

It was just a pre-glimpse of dawn
Filtering bright white off a layer of clouds.

It was that moment of calm,
Just before the storm.

It was the diamond of this morn.
Shafts of light now fan the Eastern horizon
Like beacons in the night.
As my spirit gently takes flight.

FADE TO WHITE

Golden sunrise like no other.
Watching the reflection in a tower of glass.
As orange turns to yellow
And yellow fades to white.
As the power of creation fills the morning sky.

Spirits rise ever higher
As light vanquishes darkness.
The jewels of the night's sky
Give way to the brilliant pearl of day.
Everything in a state of flux
And not an atom out of place,
As I quietly watch the chaos factor emerge triumphant!

BE FREE

You must be free to express you *own* *truth* and *passion*.

EVERYTHING

I gave you everything I had to give,
But it wasn't enough.

I turned my world upside down for you,
But it wasn't right.

I lived in a fantasy world.
You still had to live in yours.
But I still feel you in my heart.

You want only happiness for me as I wish for you.
But I still hold on to a shared vision.

I wish I had more to give you,
But I don't.

Now I have to work my way out of the fantasy.
Now I have to work my way through the confusion.
Now I have to accept my choices.
Now all I have is my Faith and Trust in the Process of Life.

IT'S EASY TO SEE

A little Belief will lift your Spirits
But a little Faith will fill your Soul!
Belief is of the Mind.
Faith is of the Heart.
And Trust is Your Choice.

IT IS

It is beyond any movie.
It is beyond virtual reality.
It is the ever-changing face of God.
It is breath for the Heart.
It is life for the Soul.
It is creation's Dance.
It is the reflection of our true nature.
It is but another sunrise morn!

It is absolutely positively, incredibly,
brilliant and magnificent!
It stops the heart and overwhelms the soul.
And all you can do is silently slip into the moment,
While compassionately embraced by the Infinite.

NO OTHER WAY

It's like four really good friends that
always go to concerts together.
Then, one of them finally learns
how to play an instrument,
And the others can't wait to be with their
buddy who plays their kind of music.

But once he learns how to play,
He plays what he feels,
Not what he used to listen to.
I don't know any other way to be,
Than the way I am!

Can you show real respect for your brothers and sisters without a condescending attitude?

DREAMS ARE ONLY FOR DREAMERS

Dreams are only for dreamers.
And *hope* is only for those
Who have something to believe in.
And when *hope is gone,*
Sad songs say so much.

ALIGNMENT WITH THE INFINITE

How do we put into words,
The pain of our hearts?
When our most cherished desires go unfulfilled.
When we struggle between the human and Divine.
When we wrestle between our wants and needs.
When will we learn to let go of the struggle
and allow true balance to stabilize our lives?
That day...when we simply handle
our every day problems
with faith and good cheer,
As we align our will with the Infinite's.

Dennis Nicomede

LOOK

Look to the skies...
Look to the trees...
Look to the other faces...
Look within!

Find the *Source* of all Love
In everything you see and feel.
Spirit lives in the energy of life.

See it
Move like the flowers and grasses of the valley

Feel it
As the rain falls gently upon your face

See it
In the play of a child

Feel it
Like a mother's touch

See it
In the shine of your lover's eyes

Feel it
As you sit alone in the dark

Look to the skies...

Look Within...

THE SEA OF GLASS

From world to world
They need this sea of glass,
To communicate with each other.
All we need are the eyes of one to another.
All we need do to be with the Father
Is *Look Within.*
Just simply, *Look Within.*
And Listen,
And Listen,
And Listen.

Love that doesn't get a chance to live,

Never dies.

That's poetry.

That's Truth!

THE ONE TRICK PONY

Honey, this is wonderful!
This is like a release of the animals at the zoo.
We don't want to be a one-trick pony.
We're one-trick ponies right now.
We keep doing the same things over
and over, and over and over.

We want to be the rainbow creatures of creation.
We want to create in every moment.
Share joy in every moment.
Give thanks in every moment.
And since we can only do one per moment,
it doesn't matter what it is that we express.
Let's just keep expressing it!
And in that expression, we shall find the Truth.
We shall find Joy.
We shall find Peace.
We shall find Happiness.
We shall find Hope beyond Hope, in this ocean of Love.

IT'S A MYSTERY

Don't try to figure out the mystery.
It's a mystery!
First it's a Spiritual path.
Know the path of the Divine through Faith.
We must make time to allow the everyday foreground
To move to the background,
And allow Spirit,
Who we have pushed into the background,
To become the foreground through Awareness –
Both conscious and in meditation.

KISSED BY THE LIGHT

Raining down her brilliant purity on this full-faced night
As the magic of smoke rings drift by
Encircled by golden rainbows
Awash in endless waves of eternal peace
Casting shadows and forming shapes
Casting spells of visionless truth.

Embraced in her reflective love
I find myself alive in this eternal moment.
Kissed by her light, I fall under her spell
As angels carry me home
Giving back that which was given to me.
With fullness of heart
I quietly bow my head to the Creator of all.

GOOD MORNING HONEY

I look at you and see myself.
I look at you and see a wonderful partner.
I look at you and see my healing.
I look at you and see pure light.
I look at you and see the Infinite.
I look at you and see Love.

My humble heart I share in return.

Any Thought of Love Unexpressed,
May be Love Felt,
But is also Love Lost!

DINING ON LOVE

Two beautiful pools of aqua blue
Soaking up the falling rain,
As I dine on the love shining bright
from her aqua blue eyes.

Her sweet honesty, innocence and truth fill my spirit,
As her touch fills my body.
Her willingness to share her love and fears so openly,
Overwhelms my very being.

I just sit and pray to be all that I can
As we share the healing power in the great Now!

AN EMERALD MORN

Pale yellow clouds extend across this emerald morn.
Worship wells deep from the core of my soul,
As the image of life comes alive.

THE WELL

It's about the living waters.

The living waters come from the deep well.

The deep well *of human and divine love,*
Of human and divine kindness,
Of human and divine goodness.

Drink deeply from the well of this life,
For every moment makes the next moment
either sweeter or more bitter.

The choice, of course, is always ours.
But it always seems to be easier,
It seems to flow better,
It seems to feel deeper when we drink from
the well of our own living heart—
When we sit in the spirit of the Divine,
When we see the overwhelming beauty,
When we feel the incredible
goodness – one to another.
When we become bathed in the light of Truth.

I toast you well on this day of days to drink
deeply from the living waters of life.

WHO REALLY FEELS IT?

Everyone feels it.
But who really feels it?
You know, deep within
From that place of knowing.
Man like child – child like man.
Who amongst us will stand up for it?
Woman like child – child like woman.
Who'll feel free enough to follow it?
Universal child – child of the universe.
Who'll trust enough to follow it?
Soldiers of the day, soldiers of the night.
Who'll be strong enough to lay their weapons down?
Never to look back.
Ever on the wing.
Everyone feels it.
But who really feels it?

It's not what position we end up coming in on,
It's the effort given and the insight
received during that process.

SURFING THE TIMELINE

Surfing the timeline is truly more than virtual reality.
It is playing the scales of life with
each passing moment.
It is the awareness of self, dissolving into the High Self.
As the material world gives way to spiritual vistas,
And our longing for union is the
drumbeat we must follow,
As a salmon returns to spawn,
As a newborn suckles for life,
So we too, must seek our Divine source.

THE WAVE

See it build—
The wave.
The incredible wave of life.
As we stand on the beautiful shore of the now,
We can watch the coming and swelling of the future
in the mounting wave
Until it rises to its perfection
And crests into the past.
The incredible pattern of Life itself
Played out every moment of every day
In metaphor after metaphor.
To the pulse of the ocean
The flapping of a butterfly's wings
The shyness of a child
The beat of our own hearts
The pattern of life
The wave of life
Life as a wave in time
Ever beckoning the future
As the past slips away into the now!

COLORS OF THE DAY

Colors of the day.
Colors of the night.
What are the colors of true insight?

What's to be questioned?
What's to be learned?

How do you listen?
How do you discern?

What position do you play?
What position would you choose?

Who would you help?
Who would you burn?
Who would you Love?
Who'll love you in return?
Who Will?

Colors of the Day.
Colors of the Night.
What are the colors of true insight?

ON THIS SUNRISE DAY

Outlines of white
Against an emerging sea of blue.
As I watch the breath of life
Breathe in a new day.
Like the webbing of a spider
Threads of transparent white penetrate the sky.

I'm overwhelmed in its silent power
As the heavens open up before me without a sound.
Soft shapes change before my eyes
As a flock of winged creatures show new directions.
Low lying haze parts as the curtains of a play
To reveal the Master Player
On this sunrise day.

TOUCHED FROM WITHIN

Brilliant moon sitting high
Awash in whiteness from the sky.
Ageless wonder,
Timeless companion.
How easily you free me from myself
And lead me through secret paths,
To the only place where the unknown can be known.
Motionless and without a word,
You compress all eternity into a moment.

The eternal reaches out and touches me from within.
I explode into a million moments.
I sit on the precipice of forever,
As one about to jump over the crest of a huge wave.
Not knowing what's going to happen
But Divinely anticipating the experiences
of but the next moment.
My heart opens to sweetly sing the praises of God.

QUESTIONS AND ANSWERS

On this moonless night
Standing under a canopy of mist,
The eternal questions are asked and re-asked.

Answers filtered through my experience with life
Yet – Higher voices beckon to keep my sanity alive.
Relearning the lessons that have never been learned,
Being able to be at peace in the
knowingness of the true God.
To trust the Master Play as it plays itself out.
In the knowledge from within,
To experience the joy from without.
To see the spark of God
Reflected in the eyes of every enlivened soul.
To see the dimness in those in pain
And those that live in fear and worry inside.
To see those that dance in the
shadows and live in the dark.
On this moonless night under a sky of mist,
Truths shall rise and fall
Like the waves of the ocean
And beyond each shadow lie some ancient wisdom
That beckons us home like a beckon in the night
Yet – it's done completely without sight.

I open my heart and mind on this moonless night
To greater visions and depths of clarity,

For greater truth, beauty and goodness
For a greater sense of worth
And peace
And harmony with the Infinite.

On this moonless night under a sky of mist
Comes the depth of being
Through the soft rhythms of universal harmony.
Comes yet another soul seeking its way home
As truth ripples through eternity
As my joy turns to love
As my love turns to wisdom
And my wisdom turns to worship
As I quietly sit on this moonless night.

SUNSET 8090

Red beams of light cleansing the
never-ending sands of time.
Small strips of aqua blue bid farewell to this day.
Waves of purple haze have the last say,
As my heart rings out with joy.

Amen.

MY LOVE WAS...

Well, as you can see,
I loved her.
I really loved her.
As I read these poems again,
I can feel how deep my love was.
I can see how childish my love was.
I can see how foolish my love was.

And now all I can say is
That my love was!

In truth.

Meditation is the practice or state
Where a quiet mind and an open heart
Can embrace the fullness of God.

CAUGHT IN THE MIDDLE

Caught in the middle—
It's that shadow feeling
Of also being caught in the middle
between the human and Divine.
Between the Spirit and the sinner
Between the thought and the action
Between the desire and the fact
Between the honor and duty
Between the past and the morrow
Just sitting waiting for an answer.
An answer that can only be answered by choice.
Caught in the middle.
Knowing the will to follow but lacking of effort,
Keeps me caught in the middle.

WISDOM OF THE AGES

Purple waves of particles
Give way to the new day's dawn.
They stream across the sky
Likes waves of love and sorrow.
Silhouetted mountain contrasts valleys below
While darkened skies fade to blue
And all seems perfect between me and you.

The wisdom of the ages ripples before me
As I look deep inside for the answers true.
Trees begin to bend and glisten
As wind begins to fill the silence.
A baby cries and a dog barks
As a smile breaks out across God's face.

STRENGTH & LOVE

There's great strength in doing everything by yourself.

But there's always love when you
do it with somebody else.

PARADISE MOMENT

The true pearl of life can be found
Watching the formless take shape
In the magic of smoke
In the flame of a fire
Or the depth of your heart,
As our Spirit rises even higher
In this paradise moment.

Your spirituality is your passion.

IN THE SPIRIT OF

In the spirit of.

Why do you ask me such things?

Why it's in the spirit of love and light.
In the spirit of truth and beauty.
In the spirit of goodness and reflective shine.
In the spirit of giving and the spirit of life.

It's in the spirit of that which was given to us.
It's in the spirit of that which we strive for.
It's in the spirit of God
And the spirit of God lights us.

That's what I mean when I say,
In the spirit of.

SILENT CALLINGS

Just one look at its brightness,
Its depth of clarity,
Its total purity
Sweeps my soul away as gently and effortlessly
As the patterns of clouds are carried away
by the unseen winds of change.
Wanting to float forever in the moment
Just as the current of love forever draws us home.
I stand motionless in its magic
Listening to its silent callings.

THE PHOENIX

She calls to my spirit with her light.
She fills my soul and beckons me home.
Rainbow shimmerings fade
As her purity fills the heavens.
A sense of peace and universal
attachment fills my being,
As I simply stand and watch the river run.

You cure through song

Calling forth the spirits

Bringing thoughts to form.

ON THE EDGE

Half moon rising on the edge of a Western storm.
Days of rain and cold lay ahead
Yet warmth grows in my heart for this
moment of sweet reflection.

And in the midst of ever-changing patterns,
I find myself falling ever deeper into my surrender—
An even sweeter connection to all life.
Breathing in the moisture-laden air,
My being feels cleansed and renewed.
I open my heart to the world
And my soul to You, Dear Lord,
My soul to You.

Half moon rising on the edge of a Western storm.

A NEW ALLEGIANCE

Rise above statehood.
Rise above nationalism.
Become a universal citizen
Borne out of the Spirit and elevated by mind.

Pledge allegiance to the seed
that binds us all together,
In the beautiful reality of brotherhood,
Seeds of the same tree—
Mothers and fathers,
Brothers and sisters are we all.

Join with us on this day
To the deeper understanding and
greater striving for world peace
By becoming a Universal citizen.

BEFORE ME IN THE FLAME

It truly is the jewel of the night sky.
An inspiration and guiding light,
Reflecting the deeper nature of God.
And there before me in the flame
Rode the wild buffalo with the bird of hope flying high.
There was the face of my lover,
brother, sister and parents
The caterpillar and butterfly.
As I looked deep in the dragon's eye
And looking deeper still,
I saw only the reflection of the "I" looking at "I,"
As in the eye of the storm.
And with chaos everywhere
I'm sweetly held in the care of my soul.

When overwhelmed by it all
Don't trouble yourself with trying to figure it out.
The answers will come as the process unfolds.
Just let it flow.

WHICH WAY HOME?

To sit and relax
To let go of all worries and doubts
To free yourself from yourself
To open yourself to Divine mind
To open yourself to a Higher Spirit
To relax your view and look deep within
To listen only to that gentle wind blowing
through the fields of your mind
To know the exquisite balance between
thought and action
The acceptance of your developing perfection in time
As you peacefully stand in the quiet silence of eternity.

Just as Spirit gives rise to God,

So do elves give rise to magic!

THE LEADING

Never fail to keep your ears open to higher resonances
Keep your heart open to higher harmony
And always keep your Spirit open
To the calling of the Eternal Spirit.

Your *Faith* shall surely be rewarded.

Your *Ax* will only result in more confusion.

It all has to do with timing
And the need to nurture or be nurtured.
It has to do with choices and perspectives.

Truth can be understood in the printed word
But truth can only be felt from one to another.

And know that when we speak to ourselves,
We speak to all creation.

A rose, is a rose, is a rose.

Just as *Truth* is timeless.

SUNRISE 103

Beautiful golden orange glow turning to yellow,
Rising in the Eastern morn
Slips up from the horizon
To illuminate another sunrise.

The slowly emerging white ripping apart night
While peeling back the darkness with its healing light.

Stars begin to fade
As sister moon begins to dim before
your motionless eyes.
Landscape forms begin to take shape as if by magic.

There's never another dawn like the one you're in.

A CRY IN THE NIGHT

Standing under a night-filled sky and thinking of her.
Overwhelmed with gratitude.
Choked up with thanks.
Overtaken by the Spirits.
Overflowing with tears.

Can't she hear me?
Doesn't she know?
I'm calling out
And can't let go!

Sitting in silence
Just reflecting my being.
It's only a matter of time before her ring
will break the stillness of night.

You must go right from an intense situation
into total silence
To have much more than a clue.

Love without action is the ruin of the soul.

ABOUT THE AUTHOR

Dennis Nicomede is just another spiritual seeker. He was born in the Los Angeles area, grew up in Orange County, California, was a CID Investigator for the Army, father of two beautiful children and a lover of life in all its forms. Always has his heart been open to the human condition and the great need for love and understanding.

He now resides with his loving wife and partner in a wonderful part of Southern Oregon known as, "The Mythical State of Jefferson" – a state of mind and place where dreams become a reality and reality becomes the dream.

Printed in the United States
138925LV00002B/2/P